Interactive Mathematics Program®

Integrated High School Mathematics

IMP

YEARS 1-2

More Problems of the Week

Dan Fendel

Key Curriculum Press
Innovators in Mathematics Education

This material is based upon work supported by the National Science Foundation under award number ESI-0137805. Any opinions, findings, and conclusions or recommendations expressed in this publication are those of the author and do not necessarily reflect the views of the National Science Foundation.

Key Curriculum Press
1150 65th Street
Emeryville, CA 94608
510-595-7000
editorial@keypress.com
http://www.keypress.com

Printed in the United States of America
10 9 8 7 6 5 4 3 2 1   08 07 06 05 04 03
ISBN 1-55953-658-6

Project Editor:
Joan Lewis

Editorial Assistant:
Lori Dixon

Consultants:
Lynne Alper
Matt Bremer
Sherry Fraser
Diane Resek

Production Director:
Diana Jean Ray

Production Editors:
Debbie Cogan
Stephanie Tanaka

Copyeditor:
Joan D. Saunders

Production Coordinator:
Charice Silverman

Text Designer:
John Ritland

Compositor:
Publication Services

Illustrator:
Evangelia Philippidis

Technical Artist:
Jason Luz

Art and Design Coordinator:
Kavitha Becker

Cover Photo Credit:
Hillary Turner

Prepress and Printer:
Data Reproductions

Executive Editor:
Casey FitzSimons

Publisher:
Steven Rasmussen

Contents

Year 2 Blackline Masters 47

•*Introduction*

This booklet contains two sets of problems, each with teacher notes, that can serve as alternative Problems of the Week (POWs) for Years 1 and 2 of the Interactive Mathematics Program® (IMP™).

POWs have been an integral part of IMP from the start. They provide students with the opportunity for open-ended exploration and analysis of mathematical situations. They also provide students with the opportunity to improve their ability to communicate about mathematics, both orally and in writing.

Most POWs are outside the main current of the unit in which they appear, and the mathematics they involve is usually not needed elsewhere in the curriculum. Therefore, it is not essential (or even expected) that all students find complete solutions or deal with all aspects of these problems. The goal is for each student to get what he or she can from the problem, including expanding his or her ability to cope with open-ended tasks and learning to persevere when the solution is not immediately in sight. In particular, we urge teachers to be cautious about giving away too much in the attempt to get students closer to the solutions.

Where to Use the Problems

The teacher commentary that accompanies the problems provides suggestions about where each POW might be used within the IMP curriculum. Some of these problems are intended specifically as possible replacements for POWs that have "gone stale" (perhaps because the solution methods have been handed down from class to class). Others are follow-ups to specific POWs in the student textbook and are intended to take the ideas of those POWs even further. Many of the problems here involve ideas that are not part of current POWs, and some are closely related to ideas within specific units. Also, you may want to use some of the problems in this collection as honors tasks rather than as POWs for the whole class.

The Hints

For every problem, the teacher commentary includes a section of hints. These are intended both to help the teacher understand and solve the problem and to provide information for the teacher to use in assisting students. As we already noted, we recommend caution in giving hints, lest they detract from students' development of independence and perseverance. Generally, you should give students at least a few days to work on a problem before offering hints, and even then, your hints should be suited to a particular student's needs.

The Solutions (or Lack of Them)

This guide does not provide solutions to these problems except in a few cases. This is done both in the belief that teachers need the same experience of struggling with a problem that students need and in the belief that there is nothing wrong with a teacher saying "I don't know" in response to students' questions.

The IMP network is always available for consultation when teachers are perplexed about whether student work is correct or when teachers need ideas about how to extend or enhance student understanding. Contact your local IMP Regional Center for further information. To find your regional center, go to www.mathimp.org.

Teacher Commentary, Year 1 POWs

POW A: *Polyominoes*

This problem can be used at any point in the IMP curriculum. It requires students to be very systematic in their work and is likely to challenge some students' ability to visualize transformations of geometric figures, especially flips. For instance, some may not easily see why the two tetrominoes shown are considered the same.

Although this POW does not involve formal work with area, the experience of exploring it may be valuable when students do study area because the problem involves the process of counting squares and illustrates that figures with the same area can have different shapes and even different perimeters.

When you introduce this problem, you might suggest that students use some type of physical representation. Objects that can be attached to each other to form polyominoes are particularly helpful because students would be able to turn and flip their creations easily. Cubes that snap together are a good option, although using three-dimensional cubes to represent two-dimensional squares could cause some confusion. Students can use objects of two distinct colors to study checkerboard polyominoes.

Be sure students understand what is meant by "the same shape." You may want to go over the case of the two tetrominoes shown and discuss why they are considered the same. You might also note that some polyominoes have two distinct colorings whereas others have only one possible coloring. For example, reversing the colors on a checkerboard domino creates a checkerboard domino that is the same as the original.

Hints

Here are two approaches that you might suggest if students have trouble developing a system for finding all the polyominoes of a given size.

- Use the set of polyominoes of a given size as the starting point for finding those of the next size. For instance, every tetromino can be formed by adding one more square to one of the two triominoes.

- Sort polyominoes by their longest straight section. For instance, in looking for pentominoes, start with the five-in-a-row pentomino. Then consider pentominoes that have a four-in-a-row but no five-in-a-row. Then look for those that have a three-in-a-row but no four-in-a-row, and so on.

In either approach, students will need to be careful to avoid repetition. Once they have all the plain polyominoes of a given size, they can explore the possible colorings to find the checkerboard polyominoes.

The number of distinct pentominoes or checkerboard pentominoes is quite manageable, so diligent and persistent students should be able to find them all, without repetition. Finding all the hexominoes is more challenging but still reasonable for a determined student. The number of plain hexominoes is between 30 and 40. We leave it to you to find the exact value. There is no known formula for the number of polyominoes in terms of the size.

Further Comments

If students consider larger polyominoes, they may wonder whether a polyomino is allowed to circle back on itself, creating holes inside. For instance, they may want to know if this figure is considered a legitimate octomino (counting just the shaded squares as being the polyomino).

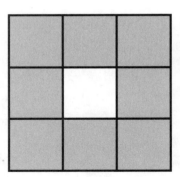

If this issue comes up, you can resolve it however you like—there is no standard definition—but students should distinguish between this figure as an octomino and the filled-in version containing nine squares in a 3-by-3 arrangement.

POW B: *Magic Squares*

You can assign this problem at any point in the curriculum. On some level, it requires nothing more than arithmetic. But some aspects can be treated in a considerably more sophisticated way than guess-and-check arithmetic. The not-completely-magic options in Questions 5b and 5c allow students to be partially successful even if they are unable to solve the problem completely.

Because magic squares are a well-known topic, some students may find online information about them. Be sure they realize that they need to do more in their write-ups than present numerical solutions.

Introducing the Problem

One way to introduce the problem is by presenting a partly magic square for the 2-by-2 case. In this figure, for instance, the sum is the same for each of the two rows, but the column sums and diagonal sums are different.

Be sure students recognize that in the 2-by-2 case, there are six distinct sums that they need to work with (two rows, two columns, and two diagonals).

1	4
2	3

Question 5 does not introduce any new ideas, but the challenge of working with a larger example will test students' perseverance. As with the 3-by-3 case, there are many solutions. You might display all the solutions that students produce so they can reflect on the variety that is possible.

Be sure students realize that they can work on Question 6 even if they have not actually found a completely magic square. You might suggest that they use a symbolic solution like the one shown here. Tell students to assume that the required sums (such as $a + b + c + d$) are equal. They should then explore how they might rearrange the letters so the result still gives equal sums.

a	b	c	d
e	f	g	h
i	j	k	l
m	n	o	p

Hints

You might suggest that students begin their work on the 3-by-3 case by trying to determine what the sums need to be. So that students know they can't try every option in their search for a solution, you might mention that there are hundreds of thousands of ways (362,880 ways, to be exact) to place the nine numbers in the nine boxes if there are no conditions on the sums.

You may want to emphasize that in Question 2, students are supposed to find *all* the solutions for the 3-by-3 case. Unlike solutions to some other problems, solutions to this problem that are not identical are considered distinct, even if they are simply rotations or flips of one another. You or students might use Question 3 to explore issues of symmetry.

You might also point out that there is some overlap between Question 3 and the second aspect of Question 1. Students can draw on the insights they came up with when working on Question 1 to justify their list from Question 2.

Presentations

When students present their work, be sure the discussion goes beyond the presentation of solutions and includes their process and their general insights. For instance, in Question 3, be sure students explain how they can be certain that each sum is 15 and how they can determine the number in the center without trial and error. In Question 4, try to elicit a variety of explanations for why a 2-by-2 magic square is impossible.

As an extension, you might encourage students, on this and similar problems, to consider other options for the set of numbers used in filling in the grid. For instance, what if they used the numbers 0 through 8 instead of 1 through 9 in the 3-by-3 case? How would the solutions in that case be related to the solutions using 1 through 9?

POW C: *Crossing the Bridge*

You can use this problem at any time. Because it has a solution that, once found, is easy to state, you may prefer to use it simply as a supplemental problem rather than as a POW. On the other hand, proving that they have found the absolute minimum will probably be a serious challenge for most students.

Hints

Many who work on this problem believe that the minimum amount of time is 19 minutes, even after they have worked on it for a while. (Some intuitions about the situation are hard to shake.)

After giving students some time with the problem, you may want to tell them that the optimal solution is less than 19 minutes. The number of available options is fairly small, so students might consider trying every possibility, no matter how counterintuitive some options may seem.

If you want to give a further hint, you might suggest that students try to minimize the amount of walking that the slow walkers do.

Further Comment

The challenge to find all the possible minimal solutions provides additional complexity. Also, this problem gives students good practice at describing the process they used to arrive at their solution and what obstacles they faced before getting to it.

POW D: *Magic Triangles*

This problem, like *POW B: Magic Squares,* requires "only" computation and can be used at any stage in the curriculum. But it has some wrinkles that are particularly challenging. For instance, as noted, different solutions to Question 1 can have different sums. Also, the *Extensions* part of the write-up, which asks students to make up their own problem, considerably expands the scope.

Introducing the Problem

On Question 1, be sure students understand that different solutions can involve different sums (unlike the situation in *POW B: Magic Squares*). Challenge students to find as many different solutions as they can, then to justify how they know that they have all the solutions, or at least all the possible sums. Tell students they need not give every solution, but suggest that they describe how to get other solutions from the ones they have. For instance, they might note that in any solution, they can switch the two middle numbers along any given side and get another solution.

Question 2 is definitely more difficult, and you may want to assure students that there are solutions. Be sure they know that the six outer numbers must give the same sum as each of the four-in-a-row sides.

You might explicitly mention the make-up-your-own component of the *Extensions* part of the write-up.

Hints

On Question 1, you might point out that the three vertex circles are counted twice if the sums for the three sides are added together. This may help students see why different sums are possible, depending on what numbers are placed in the vertex circles. You might suggest that they consider different options for the three vertex circles and determine in each case what the sum for each side would have to be. Doing this may help them see a condition that must be true about the numbers in the three vertex circles.

There are five possibilities for the common sum. Two other potential common sums turn out not to yield any solutions. You might alert students that considerable trial and error is needed to find all the solutions.

Question 2 has six different solutions, aside from variations based on symmetry. Finding them all is a genuine challenge. You can suggest that students begin by figuring out what the sum must be for each of the six sets of four-in-a-row circles (as asked in part a). As a further hint, you could bring out that each circle—and hence each number from 1 through 12—is part of exactly two of the four-in-a-row sums.

Once students determine this common sum, the options for the six numbers in the vertices will be considerably limited. Students might find it helpful to have a diagram like the one in the problem, showing the 12 circles, and 12 markers, numbered 1 through 12, to move around as they search for a solution.

Presentations

In discussing Question 1, challenge students to prove they have all the possibilities for the common sum, or tell them there are others if they haven't found them all.

If students don't find a solution to the double-triangle problem, you can leave it as an open question. If they do find solutions, you might ask if they notice anything about the sum of each triangle's vertices. If they have noticed a property, ask them to look for a reason why this property must hold.

If students include their own problems in the *Extensions* part of their write-ups, you might have them exchange and work on each other's problems.

POW E: *Tic-Tac-Toe and Friends*

This problem, like *POW 6: Linear Nim,* in *The Game of Pig,* involves analyzing a game and developing a strategy. It can be used at any time in the IMP curriculum. Questions 1, 2a, and 3a are perhaps simpler than *POW 6: Linear Nim,* but Question 2b is complex, and writing a complete exposition for Question 3b is probably more difficult than analyzing the generalizations suggested in *POW 6: Linear Nim.* You might decide that Question 1 presents sufficient challenge for your students and assign that by itself.

Although many of your students may have played tic-tac-toe, they may not have given much thought to a detailed analysis of the game, and few will have studied the variations, so this problem has much to offer in a familiar setting.

Introducing the Problem

For students who have not played tic-tac-toe, you should allow some opportunity for them to mess around with the game. This is a good problem for students to work on in pairs, so you might ask students to find a partner and play the game.

If students have not worked on *POW 6: Linear Nim* or other strategy problems, you should take some time to discuss what a complete strategy is. Students should indicate in their write-ups which player (if any) can guarantee a win and should be explicit about how a given player should play or respond to each option the other player has.

Because Questions 2b and 3b are complex, students may not be able to give a full analysis of these situations. Encourage them to give as complete an answer as they can.

Comment: Question 3a is, in a sense, repetitive of Question 2a, but the two are framed differently. Students who have trouble with Question 2a may want to go back to it after working on Question 3a.

Hints

You might bring out that going first cannot possibly be a disadvantage in these games because having an extra mark on the board can't hurt. Therefore, the first player should never do any worse than achieve a tie. So the student's goal is either to show that **X** can guarantee a win or to show that **O** can prevent **X** from winning. Based on this insight, you might suggest that students follow their intuition about which goal is likely to be achievable.

Encourage students to use ideas of symmetry in helping analyze the possibilities. For instance, for regular tic-tac-toe, they can see that **X**'s opening move is one of three types—a corner square, a side square, and the center square. If needed, help students see that each corner square is just like every other corner square and each side square is just like every other side square.

Similarly, if **X** starts in a corner, **O** has five distinct responses to consider (adjacent side, adjacent corner, nonadjacent side, opposite corner, and center), even though there are eight open squares.

Students can use the same sort of ideas to simplify things in Question 2, as the hint suggests. They might decide to pursue in detail a particular part of the problem—for instance, the case where **X** starts in the upper left. They may need to make an intuitive choice as to whether to try to show that **X** can win or to try to show that **O** can prevent **X** from winning.

In Question 3, where the board is unlimited, the location of **X**'s first move really doesn't matter.

Although Question 3b asks about four in a row, it turns out that on an unlimited board the first player can actually play in such a way that he or she cannot be prevented from getting *five* in a row. For more about this, see the discussion about the game Go Maku under "Further Variations."

Presentations

One important element of students' presentations is that the strategy they put forward must be clear and complete. To demonstrate whether this has been accomplished, you might have a student other than the presenter(s) try to follow the proposed strategy.

You may wind up leaving complex parts of this problem unresolved. There is no reason to give students a solution (if you have one) because they don't need the answer at any point in the curriculum.

Further Variations

For students who are intrigued by tic-tac-toe, here are some related games that they might explore.

- Reverse tic-tac-toe: This variation uses the regular 3-by-3 tic-tac-toe grid, but a player who gets three in a row is the *loser.*

- Three-dimensional tic-tac-toe: This variation uses a 4-by-4-by-4 cube, and each move consists of putting a marker in one of the 64 cells that make up the cube. A player wins by getting four marks in a row. The four-in-a-row can be formed in many directions, including different types of diagonals, so visualizing all the possible wins may be difficult. Commercial and online versions of this game are available, although students may be able to play with four adjacent 4-by-4 squares, using their imagination to visualize the various straight lines that would occur in the three-dimensional version.

- Go Maku (also called Go Bang): This game, of Japanese origin, requires a player to get five marks in a row. As noted in an earlier comment, if no extra rules are added to the basic idea of tic-tac-toe, the first player can force a win. Therefore, to make the game more interesting, Go Maku imposes the special restriction that a player is not allowed to create two sets of three in a row that are each open at both ends. The game is often played on a 19-by-19 board.

- Tic-tac-toe on a cylinder or Möbius strip: You can find interactive versions of these tic-tac-toe variations for two students or one student against the computer online at www.keypress.com/space.

POW F: *Crossing Old Rivers*

These puzzles can be used at any time; they are similar in flavor to *Crossing the Bridge*. If you use them simply as supplemental problems, you can assign them one at a time rather than as a set.

Part of the appeal with this POW is the recognition that puzzles such as these have been around for a very long time yet still can be perplexing.

Introducing the Problem

In problems such as these, students often have questions about the rules for solving the problem. For instance, on Question 1 you may want to clear up issues such as: "Can the women row?" (Yes.) "Can people swim back and forth?" (No.) "Can someone hang on to the boat while two other people are in it?" (No.) In general, tell students that they do not need any tricks to solve these problems.

Hints

You may want to suggest that students use materials—even as simple as slips of paper—to represent the various people or objects and to act out the scenarios. If students are stuck, point out that there are a limited number of options to consider at each stage and that they can always simply try everything.

You might also emphasize to students that they should try to demonstrate that they have solved each problem using the fewest possible steps.

● POW G: *Exposed*

This problem is similar to but considerably harder than the supplemental problem *Painting the General Cube,* in *The Overland Trail.* You can assign this problem after students have had some experience developing formulas or rules for complex situations. You might use *Painting the General Cube* as a preparatory problem.

Introducing the Problem

In introducing this problem, be sure students recognize that the figure includes many hidden stones. You might clarify to the whole class, for instance, that the bottom layer contains 49 stones (7 · 7) and so on. Also, be sure that students know the meaning of the term *face* (first used in Question 2) and that they realize every exposed face gets wet.

You may want to have objects (such as cubes that snap together) available for students to use in creating physical models of the situation, although they probably will not want to build these structures beyond the smallest examples.

You may want to warn students that the *Super Challenge* is quite difficult and that they may not yet have the background to find a solution (but see the comments further on).

Hints

On Question 1, students may start out by counting the exposed stones layer by layer. That's fine, but urge them to look for a simpler way. If they examine the number of exposed stones for pyramids of different heights, the results should form a familiar pattern, which may give them some insight about a shortcut. Urge them not only to find the shortcut but also to explain why it is correct.

Question 2 is more geometric than algebraic, and students may find a physical model helpful.

Question 3 begins the process of generalization, even though it involves a specific case. Students will certainly not want to build the structure described here (which would require thousands of individual cubes) and probably won't even want to sketch it in detail, so they will need to look for patterns to explain what happens. If students are having difficulty with Question 3, you might suggest that they look at an in-between case, such as a structure in which the bottom layer is 13-by-13.

For Question 4, there are several aspects for generalization. You might point out that the general structure involves square arrays at each layer with an odd number of stones along each edge and suggest that students look for various formulas for the structure with N layers. They can seek formulas for the size of the bottom layer, the number of exposed stones, and the number of stones with a given number of exposed faces, all expressed in terms of the number of layers.

The Super Challenge

For the *Super Challenge,* a first stage for students is seeing how to write the total number of stones as a sum. For instance, the total number of stones in the four-layer structure shown is $1^2 + 3^2 + 5^2 + 7^2$. If students see this, urge them to write the number of stones for the *N*-layer structure in summation notation (using *N* as the upper limit of the sum). This in itself would be a worthwhile achievement.

A deeper challenge is to find a closed formula. This is quite difficult, although there is a polynomial expression giving the number of stones in terms of the number of layers. You may choose to leave this as an open challenge.

Here are two approaches you might suggest to students who want to pursue this.

- The summation approach: Students may be familiar with a formula for the sum of the first *N* positive integers. (See the *Patterns* supplemental problem *From One to N.*) Here they are looking for a formula for the sum of the first *N* odd squares. You might suggest that they do some research on such formulas. The formula for the sum of the first *N* positive squares is well known, and students may be able to find this formula in a textbook. Students with good skills at algebra manipulations might be able to adjust this formula to get the sum of the first *N* odd squares.

- The data-search approach: In this method, students explore by gathering data and looking for patterns. They can start with an In-Out table such as this.

Number of layers	Total number of stones
1	1
2	10
3	35
4	84
5	165

It turns out that if students look at triple the number of stones and think about writing each result as a product of three factors (which makes sense because they are working with a three-dimensional figure), they may be able to recognize a pattern. *A further hint:* If one of those factors (of the tripled value) is the number of layers, what are the other two factors?

Note: The formula for the volume of a pyramid involves a factor of $\frac{1}{3}$. The tripling suggested here essentially "undoes" that factor.

Students may not yet be able to justify any formula they get, but they might do so as their mathematical learning progresses, by using mathematical induction or by adapting known summation formulas.

POW H: *Egyptian Fractions*

Question 1 is similar in flavor to *POW 2: 1-2-3-4 Puzzle,* in *Patterns.* You might assign only Question 1 to students who need practice on fraction arithmetic. The remaining questions require careful reasoning, so you might assign them after students have had some exposure to proof, such as in *Homework 12: That's Odd!,* in *Patterns,* which involves showing that every odd whole number is a consecutive sum.

Introducing the Problem

In introducing this problem, be sure students understand the two rules.

- Use only unit fractions.

- Do not use the same unit fraction more than once in a given expression.

Questions may require additional clarification. In Question 2, for example, students may begin by looking at *specific* fractions with a numerator of 2, but their goal is to show that *any* such fraction can be written using only two terms. You might point out that Question 3 says "at most three distinct unit fractions" and that using only two also is okay.

Hints

One approach you might suggest to help students get started on Question 1 is that they list all the fractions they are trying to represent. Then simply combine various unit fractions to see what the sums are; if the sum is on their list, they can cross it off. (Students may have used a similar approach in *POW 2: 1-2-3-4 Puzzle.*)

Question 2 suggests that students start by considering specific examples and looking for patterns. But they also need to look for a general argument. Their solution might include an algorithm—that is, a general procedure for producing the two desired fractions. Encourage them to include an explanation for why their procedure always works.

Question 3 is similar to Question 2. Some students may see a way to use their result from Question 2 to answer Question 3. Encourage students to give examples even if they can't find general procedures. You might suggest that they look separately at the cases of an even denominator and an odd denominator. (The former is easier.) Question 4 is intentionally open-ended. Students should simply share the ideas they have after working on Questions 2 and 3 and other examples.

Presentations

When students present their work on Question 1, encourage them to share additional possible answers. For instance, $\frac{2}{7}$ can be written as $\frac{1}{7} + \frac{1}{14} + \frac{1}{21} + \frac{1}{42}$, but it can also be written as $\frac{1}{4} + \frac{1}{28}$ and other ways.

In Question 2, if students describe an algorithm but cannot justify it, you may want to discuss how to use algebra to represent the algorithm and to give a proof that it works. For instance, students may have started by considering these examples.

- $\frac{2}{3} = \frac{1}{2} + \frac{1}{6}$

- $\frac{2}{5} = \frac{1}{3} + \frac{1}{15}$

- $\frac{2}{7} = \frac{1}{4} + \frac{1}{28}$

They may see a pattern and be able to describe a general way to get the two fractions. As a first step, you might ask them how to get the first denominator on the right from the original denominator.

You can encourage the class to turn their ideas into algebraic form, then have them work on the algebraic manipulations needed to show that it works. An algebraic expression for the odd denominator might be $2k - 1$.

If students answer Question 3 by saying, in effect, that they can simply write $\frac{3}{N}$ as $\frac{1}{N} + \frac{2}{N}$ and can follow that with applying Question 2 to the second term, point out that they need to be sure this process will yield distinct unit fractions. Then ask them how they know this is so.

The key idea in Question 4 is that whatever your initial fraction, you can find some unit fraction such that what's left—the difference—is a fraction whose numerator is smaller than that of the original fraction. As you repeat this process, the numerator of what's left keeps going down, by at least 1 at each step. There are two details to demonstrate: First, show that at any stage you can find a unit fraction so that the difference remaining has a smaller numerator; second, show that in doing this process over and over, you don't repeat a denominator.

● POW I: *Pieces at Peace*

This problem, like *POW 12: The Big Knight Switch,* in *The Pit and the Pendulum,* is framed in terms of chess pieces and the way they move, although the main questions in this problem could be stated without any reference to chess. Like *POW 12: The Big Knight Switch,* this problem has no specific mathematical prerequisite and can be used at any time.

Questions 1 through 5 build gradually in complexity. All students should be able to answer Questions 1 through 3 fairly readily, then move on to the more challenging problems.

Introducing the Problem

In introducing this problem, be sure students understand how the queen moves and what a diagonal is in this context. You might ask students to state the problem in a more purely mathematical way, such as: "How many squares can you mark so that no two marks are in the same row, column, or diagonal?" You also may want to point out that the coloring of the checkerboard squares is not particularly relevant to this problem. Assure students that they do not need to know how to play chess to succeed with this problem.

For Question 6, you should be sure students understand the movements for the other chess pieces. You may want to suggest that they select only one of the given pieces to analyze.

Hints

It will help some students to work with movable markers. As they place a marker to represent a queen or another piece, they might use markers of a different color to indicate squares that are then under attack and cannot be used.

The solutions for Questions 1 through 5 may give students insight about solutions in the case of rooks. However, the connection between queens and the cases of bishops and knights is less simple, and there is no obvious analog to Question 1 for these cases. For bishops, you might point out that bishops can attack only pieces on squares of the same color.

Presentations

You might identify students' reasoning in Question 1 as an example of the pigeonhole principle, which says that if you need to put $N + 1$ pigeons in N pigeonholes, you will need to put at least two pigeons in the same pigeonhole. Be sure students see that Question 1 gives them only an upper bound on the number of queens that can be at peace and that the actual number possible may be fewer in specific cases. For instance, they cannot have two queens at peace on a 2-by-2 checkerboard.

POW J: *A Camel Messenger*

This problem is a variation on *POW 13: Corey Camel,* in *The Pit and the Pendulum.* You might use it either in place of that POW (for instance, if many students already know its solution) or as a follow-up to it (for instance, if students want to work on another, similar problem).

If students have not worked on *POW 13: Corey Camel,* you may want to create a simplified version, similar to *A Mini-POW About Mini-Camel,* in which Dory goes shorter distances but can carry fewer bananas.

Introducing the Problem

You might discuss how this problem is different from *POW 13: Corey Camel.*

- Dory has to make a round trip, whereas Corey went in only one direction.

- In *POW 13: Corey Camel,* students were given the initial number of bananas and needed to find out how many Corey could get to market. Here, Dory does not need to have any bananas for the market, and the task is to determine how many bananas she needs for the round trip.

Hints

In both problems, the key to the solution is to bring some bananas part way, store them, then go back for more. As a hint, you might point out that Dory can store bananas to pick up on her return trip.

Teacher Commentary, Year 2 POWs

POW A: *Last Loses and Other Nim Variations*

This problem is intended as a follow-up to *POW 6: Linear Nim,* in the Year 1 unit *The Game of Pig.* Although this problem gives the rules for the basic linear Nim game, which means it could stand on its own, we recommend that students work on *POW 6: Linear Nim* first. This problem can be used at any time after that.

Introducing the Problem

You may wish to ask students to review their work from *POW 6: Linear Nim* as an introduction to this problem. Have students play the original game (with 10 marks) at least a few times as a refresher so they see that Player 1 can win by crossing off 2 marks, then responding to Player 2's first move so the number of marks remaining is 4, and, finally, taking whatever is left after Player 2's second move. You can use this to review what a strategy is and to emphasize that a player's strategy must take into account every possible move by the other player.

You may also want to have students play Last Loses and At Least Two a few times each in class to be sure they are clear about the rules. In particular, be sure they recognize the possibility of a tie for At Least Two. For instance, if that game is played starting with only 4 marks, then Player 1 can earn a tie by crossing off 3 marks. On the other hand, there is no way for Player 1 to win this game, and if Player 1 crosses off 2 marks, then Player 2 will win.

As with other strategy problems involving two-person games, you might recommend that students work on this problem in pairs.

Hints

You can suggest that students keep track of situations in which they are sure who will win, and that they build on that information. For instance, in Last Loses, a player who has 2, 3, or 4 marks remaining at his or her turn can win by removing all but 1 mark. Therefore, 2, 3, and 4 are winning positions, and a player should avoid leaving the other player with those amounts. On the other hand, if a player has 5 marks remaining, he or she has no choice but to leave 2, 3, or 4, so 5 is a losing position.

Presentations

This problem provides students with an open-ended investigation, based on different ways to modify the game. Be sure to allow many different results to emerge when students present their work. Some students might concentrate on a detailed analysis of one type of variation, whereas others may investigate particular examples of several different variations.

POW B: *Old Number Puzzles*

Students might approach these problems either from a guess-and-check perspective or by using some basic algebra ideas. To keep the latter option open, you might assign this problem after students have worked on solving linear equations in *Solve It!*

Introducing the Problems

The language in some of these problems is a bit archaic, so you might take time to make sure students understand what is going on. For instance, you can clarify Question 1 by asking for a guess about what number is added, then following the directions of the problem to see if it gives the desired result. For example, if a student suggests 30 as the number to be added, then the resulting numbers are 130 (by adding 100 + 30) and 50 (by adding 20 + 30). Students should determine that 130 and 50 are not in the ratio 3 to 1, so 30 is not the right number to add.

Similarly, in Question 2, have a student guess what the two numbers are. If a student gives you the pair 50 and 100, ask what numbers result if "the first receives 30 from the second." Be sure they see that this means not only that the first number increases by 30 (giving 80) but also that the second number decreases by 30 (giving 70). Students can then verify that 80 and 70 are not in the ratio of 2 to 1, so the combination of 50 and 100 is not the answer to the problem.

Question 3 is similar to *POW 8: The Haybaler Problem,* in the Year 1 unit *The Overland Trail,* in that it involves finding a set of numbers so that certain "partial sums" yield certain totals that are given. Be sure students understand that "omitting each number in turn" means that 22 is the sum of all but the first number, that 24 is the sum of all but the second number, and so on.

Finally, you may want to have students read the problem in Question 4 aloud to be sure they understand what is happening. For instance, the problem asserts that Diophantos had lived $\frac{1}{6} + \frac{1}{12}$ of his life when his beard began to grow and an *additional* $\frac{1}{7}$ of his life when he married.

Hints

All of these problems can be approached using a guess-and-check method, but you may want to suggest that students try to formulate algebraic representations, then use what they have learned about working with algebraic symbols to find the answer.

The imitate-your-arithmetic approach may be helpful in creating algebraic representations. For instance, in Question 1 students can see that in the example given under "Introducing the Problems," they added 30 to both 100 and 20, then determined if the first sum was three times the second. Encourage them to translate this arithmetic into algebraic language. They should get something similar to the equation $100 + x = 3 \cdot (20 + x)$. They can then apply what they learned from *Homework 6: The Mystery Bags Game* and related activities in *Solve It!* to solve this equation.

For Question 2, this approach might lead students to a set of two equations with two variables. If so, they can use graphing to find the solution. (If they want to graph the equations on a calculator, they will first need to put them in "$y =$" form.)

There is a different hint—more of a guess-and-check method—you might offer for Question 2. Suggest students start by guessing the two numbers that represent the result after "the first receives 30 from the second" so that these two numbers must be in the ratio 2 to 1. Then they can reconstruct the original numbers and test to see what happens if "the second receives 50 from the first."

Playing around with this approach will help students see whether to adjust their original guess up or down, and they can gradually get closer to the solution. This method can also be used to formulate a one-variable equation, by labeling the "after" numbers as $2x$ and x.

If you think students need a hint for Question 3, you might lead them to an intuitive approach. Help them realize that adding the numbers three at a time gives totals between 20 and 27, which suggests that the numbers average about 8 and so are probably not far from that value.

A more analytic approach is to see that adding the four given numbers (22, 24, 27, and 20) gives a sum that uses the four unknown numbers three times each (because each number is included in three of the four sums). This insight can lead students to discover the sum of all four unknown numbers and, from there, the numbers themselves.

In Question 4, students may make an educated guess based on the expectation that the answer is a whole number and that all the parts of Diophantos's life are also whole numbers. This will likely lead to the correct solution (especially if they think about what a typical life span might be). If you notice that students are doing this, you might ask them to solve the problem with "five years after his marriage" changed to some other value. That will force them to be more systematic and algebraic in their approach.

Presentations

If students use primarily a guess-and-check approach in their presentations of these problems, you may want to prod them during the presentations to discuss how they might express their ideas in algebraic terms. Be careful to do this without suggesting that there is anything wrong with a guess-and-check approach.

POW C: *A Square in a Square*

Students can do well on this problem by working many examples, but they may be able to better understand and justify their conclusions if they have some familiarity with factoring. So we suggest that you assign this problem after students have done *A Lot of Changing Sides,* in *Solve It!,* and similar work. Alternatively, you could save this problem until after students have more experience with quadratic expressions, after the *Fireworks* unit in Year 3.

Introducing the Problem

After students have looked over the problem, you might want to have them formulate the task in explicit mathematical terms. This is part of the *Problem Statement* portion of the write-up, so you may not want to include this in a class discussion. Students should see that their task is to determine which whole numbers can be expressed as the difference between the squares of two positive integers.

Point out that Question 1 asks them to explore certain specific cases (numbers 1 through 20). Make sure they see that "1 through 20" refers to the *differences* they are trying to get, not to the possible dimensions of the squares. Question 2 asks them to find general patterns for numbers that represent areas Leslie can obtain and for those that represent areas she is unable to obtain.

The pattern of possible differences may be clearer and students may be able to reach general conclusions more readily if they allow the option that Elissa gets no space. (They can think of this as using 0 as the length of the side for Elissa's square.) If students are stuck, you might suggest that they include this option, even though it doesn't quite fit the scenario described.

Hints

If students are having trouble getting started, suggest that they simply try various combinations for the large square and the small square and see how much area Leslie has left. If they need further help, you might propose that they make a 2-input table like the one on the facing page. (The side lengths shown are those provided in the problem.)

Inputs		Output
Side of Leslie's square	Side of Elissa's square	Difference in the areas
4	2	12

If needed, have students include columns for "Area of Leslie's square" and "Area of Elissa's square." Point out that their goal is to determine what the output can be using positive integer inputs (or allowing 0 as an option for Elissa).

Once they have made such a table, they should look at which outputs are possible and which are not, then try to find patterns or rules to describe what they see. Urge students to use algebra to justify their conclusions.

Presentations

If students did not include the option of 0 for Elissa, they will likely see that 1 and 4 are exceptions to the general rule that the area remaining for Leslie can be any number that is either odd or a multiple of 4, whereas it cannot be an even number that is not a multiple of 4 (such as 2, 6, or 10). You can take this opportunity to point out that including 0 as an option for Elissa would eliminate the exceptions.

Ask if anyone found an explanation for this general rule. Students might note that the differences between successive squares are the odd positive numbers. For instance, $2^2 - 1^2 = 3, 3^2 - 2^2 = 5, 4^2 - 3^2 = 7$, and so on.

As a step toward generalizing this observation, you might ask how 73 can be written as a difference of squares. As a hint, ask what numbers were used to express 7 and how those numbers are related to 7. Students might see that 4 is just above half of 7 and that 3 is just below half of 7. This might lead to their realizing that 73 is likely to be $37^2 - 36^2$, which they can verify.

As a further step, see if students can express this algebraically, starting by writing the odd number as $2N + 1$.

Difference of Squares

If students have worked enough with factoring, they may realize that any difference of squares, $x^2 - y^2$, can be written as the product $(x + y)(x - y)$. If students are comfortable with this idea, you might use it as a hint for why numbers that are even but not multiples of 4 cannot be written in this form.

POW D: *Triangle Variety*

This problem is a follow-up to geoboard activities in *Do Bees Build It Best?* and can be used at any time after about Day 6 of that unit. You might decide that a combination of Questions 1 and 2 (or Questions 1 and 3) is sufficient challenge, saving the remaining parts for later in the curriculum.

Introducing the Problem

In introducing this problem, be sure students understand the word *congruent* and know that "a complete set of noncongruent triangles" means a set of triangles, all different (not congruent), such that every possible geoboard triangle is congruent to one of the triangles in the set. You might provide students with geoboard paper to make recording their work easier.

Hints

You might suggest that students use symmetry (which is related to congruence) to help manage the tasks of Questions 1 and 3. For instance, any triangle that has a "corner" vertex is congruent to one that has a vertex at the peg in the upper left corner. This type of reasoning will help decrease the number of cases that students need to consider.

Questions 2 and 4 may intimidate students at first. You might suggest that they consider what they need to do to specify a triangle. Basically, they need to identify the three pegs that represent the vertices, so the problem involves counting the number of combinations of pegs that give triangles.

Students might approach Question 2, which involves a 3-peg–by–3-peg geoboard, by labeling the pegs with numbers 1 through 9 and systematically listing the combinations. They might use a system like this, in which each group of three numbers represents a potential set of vertices and the groups are listed in increasing order.

Combinations using vertex 1 as the first vertex:

1, 2, 3; 1, 2, 4; 1, 2, 5; . . . ; 1, 2, 9

1, 3, 4; 1, 3, 5; 1, 3, 6; . . . ; 1, 3, 9

. . .

1, 8, 9

Combinations using vertex 2 as the first vertex:

2, 3, 4; 2, 3, 5; . . . ; 2, 3, 9

. . .

2, 8, 9

and so on through the last case, which is the single combination using vertex 7 as the first vertex:

7, 8, 9

Although considerable work is involved, students who persist should be able to determine how many cases this is. (There are fewer than 100, which makes the task tedious but manageable; we leave it to you to determine the exact number.) If students have done work with combinatorics, they may know shortcuts for counting how many such combinations there are.

But the matter is complicated by the fact that not every set of three pegs represents a triangle. For instance, the three pegs along the top row of the geoboard do not because they are collinear. Students will need to eliminate those combinations that do not represent triangles. *For your information:* There are exactly 76 distinct triangles on a 3-peg-by-3-peg geoboard.

Finding the solution to Question 4, which involves a 4-peg-by-4-peg geoboard, is a much lengthier process but still accessible for students who are willing to work through it systematically. For a 4-peg-by-4-peg geoboard, a complete set of noncongruent triangles contains 30 distinct triangles (including the 8 triangles that fit on a 3-peg-by-3-peg geoboard). There are 516 possible triangles altogether.

Presentations

You can have a student share his or her complete set of noncongruent triangles for Question 1, then see if other students have examples that were overlooked or if there are any duplications in the set. Ask the class how they determined that they had all the possibilities. Prod them to describe a systematic method rather than simply saying things like "I couldn't find any others." The complete set has 8 distinct triangles, including the small triangle that fits on a 2-peg-by-2-peg geoboard.

For Question 2, you can follow a similar process, although you may suggest that students describe *how they found* all the triangles or how they determined how many there are rather than show them all.

Students can do the presentations for Questions 3 and 4 in a similar way.

POW E: *Geoboard Squares*

This problem is related to *Homework 13: Make the Lines Count*, in *Do Bees Build It Best?*, which involves finding the different lengths on a 5-peg–by–5-peg geoboard. Although students do not need to have done that assignment before working on *Geoboard Squares*, it makes sense to assign *Geoboard Squares* as a follow-up to *Homework 13: Make the Lines Count*.

Introducing the Problem

This problem requires only a short introduction. Be sure students realize that they are to determine the *distinct* (that is, noncongruent) squares.

Hints

If needed, remind students that they should initially focus on the number of *new* squares that can be formed at each stage as the geoboard size increases. You can help them see that such squares should have their vertices along the four edges of the geoboard. (Otherwise, they could be formed on a smaller geoboard.) You can suggest as a further hint that they consider where the vertex on the upper edge might go and bring out that by symmetry they can limit their search to cases where this vertex is in the left half of that edge.

A table may help students see what's going on. The table here gives not only the number of *new* squares at a given stage (for use in Questions 1 and 2) but also the *cumulative total* at each stage (for use in Question 3).

Number of pegs per row	Number of new squares	Total number of squares
1	0	0
2	1	1
3	2	3
4	2	5
5	3	8
6	3	11

From such a table, students should be able to see the pattern for the number of new squares, but point out that for Question 2 they need to generalize and find an explanation for their generalization.

For a hint on Question 3, you might suggest that students consider separately the cases of odd numbers of pegs per row and the cases of even numbers of pegs per row. You might also suggest that they look at what would happen if they considered a single point as a square of size 0 so that the 0 entries above would become 1 (which would add 1 to all the entries in the last column). Students should pay particular attention to the totals (with this "plus 1" modification) for the cases of odd numbers of pegs per row.

Presentations

Students are likely to see the pattern that the number of new squares goes up by 1 at each odd number. For example, using n as the number of pegs per row, there is 1 new square when $n = 2$, but this goes up to 2 new squares for $n = 3$, stays at 2 for $n = 4$, goes up to 3 at $n = 5$, stays at 3 for $n = 6$, and so on. So the pattern, after the initial 0, 1, is 2, 2, 3, 3, 4, 4, 5, 5, and so on. (This pattern is another hint that considering what happens if the 0 is changed to 1 might be helpful.)

If students don't give an explanation of this pattern, try to elicit one, perhaps based on the hint mentioned earlier concerning the options for the location of the vertex along the upper edge. So if there are 5 pegs per row, there are three choices (the first, second, or third peg) that give distinct squares. But if there are 6 pegs per row, there are still only three choices. The presence of a "middle peg" for odd numbers of pegs per row leads to the additional square being possible.

Be sure to have someone illustrate how this pattern applies to large numbers, such as explaining why the 100-peg-by–100-peg geoboard yields 50 new squares.

If students do not come up with formulas or patterns for Question 3, you may choose to leave the question open. Alternatively, you might ask students to determine the total number of squares for $n = 100$. They may see that they can get this as the sum $0 + 1 + 2 + 2 + 3 + 3 + \cdots + 50 + 50$, then look for shortcuts for getting this sum.

If students follow the suggestion of changing the initial 0 to 1, they may see that this is simply twice the sum $1 + 2 + 3 + \cdots + 50$ and use any of the usual techniques to find this sum. For instance, they may see that with 0 changed to 1, the sum is $50 \cdot 51$ and use this as a clue to a generalization. As noted earlier, students should look for separate patterns for odd values of n and even values of n.

POW F: *Geoboard Triangle Areas*

This problem might serve well as a follow-up to *POW 8: Just Count the Pegs,* in *Do Bees Build It Best?,* because that POW gives a helpful shortcut for finding areas of polygons on a geoboard. In any case, it should come after students have had some experience working with such areas and have developed the formula for area of a triangle as half the product of base and height (for instance, after discussion of *Homework 6: The Ins and Outs of Area,* in *Do Bees Build It Best?*).

Introducing the Problem

You might introduce this problem by working with a 3-peg-by-3-peg geoboard and having students consider the special category of triangles that have a horizontal side.

For this special category, students should see that the base can be either 1 or 2, the height can be either 1 or 2, and the area is half of any product of two such numbers, which gives the values $\frac{1}{2}$, 1, or 2 as areas that can be achieved.

Point out that this analysis does *not* yield a triangle with area $1\frac{1}{2}$ and that the task of *Geoboard Triangle Areas* is to determine *all* the possible areas. Urge students to look for a triangle with area $1\frac{1}{2}$. They should realize that they must consider triangles with no horizontal (or vertical) side. The figure shown here (or the equivalent) is the only solution.

Be sure students understand that their task in this problem is to perform a similar analysis for larger geoboards, giving at least one example for each area that they think is possible.

For Question 5, you can suggest that students make predictions for specific cases or in general, based on their work on Questions 1 through 4. Even if they cannot prove their conclusions, however, urge them to indicate what makes them think their conclusions are true.

You may want to provide students with geoboard paper on which to record their results.

Hints

If students have successfully completed *POW 8: Just Count the Pegs*, they can use their results to deduce that all possible areas are whole-number multiples of $\frac{1}{2}$, that is, either whole numbers or $\frac{1}{2}$ plus a whole number. The challenge, then, is to see whether all such values can actually be achieved. *POW 8: Just Count the Pegs* provides a convenient way to compute areas, and students may appreciate the opportunity to use whatever formulas they developed in that POW.

Presentations

You may want to provide presenters in advance with transparencies with geoboard dots to facilitate presentations.

The maximum area for a triangle on a square geoboard is half the geoboard's total area. For an N-peg-by-N-peg geoboard, this maximum is $\frac{1}{2}(N-1)^2$. It turns out that every multiple of $\frac{1}{2}$ up to this maximum is, in fact, the area of some triangle. Perhaps more amazing (and consider this a hint), you can pick two fixed vertices (you need the right ones), then achieve all the different areas just by changing the third vertex!

POW G: *What's That Hat?*

This problem is similar to (but perhaps a bit easier than) *POW 11: A Hat of a Different Color,* in *Cookies.*

Introducing the Problem

After students have read the problem, be sure they understand that the three candidates initially do not know what color hats they have and that the candidates need to figure this out based on what they observe. As in *POW 11: A Hat of a Different Color,* the key is that their observations include the behavior of the other candidates.

Emphasize that in their write-ups students need to explain their reasoning fully and not just assert that they know their own hat must be black.

Hints

You might suggest that students consider what would happen if they got a white hat and the other two candidates got black hats. Remind students that their explanations should reflect the assumption that "the other two candidates are reasonably bright people."

Presentations

If no one has done so as an extension, you might ask the class to consider other color combinations for the hats. For instance, what would the candidates have been able to deduce (and how would they have deduced it) if all three had been given white hats? What if two hats had been white and one black? What about two black and one white?

POW H: *Sheep and Goats*

This problem is similar to *POW 13: Shuttling Around,* in *Cookies.* You might use this problem as either an alternate or a follow-up to that one.

Introducing the Problem

You may need to clarify the rules for this problem. In particular, be sure students understand that as a pair of animals is moved, they remain in their original order. That is, if the sheep is to the left of the goat, it stays to the left of the goat, and vice versa.

You might also point out that because there are always exactly two empty pens, students need say only which animals are moved at a given step and need not specify where they go.

Hints

You might suggest that students use markers, such as pennies and nickels, to represent the sheep and goats. They will probably find it helpful to develop some sort of system for recording their work. For instance, they can record a move by stating which pens are emptied.

Presentations

After presenters have given methods of accomplishing the switches described in Questions 1 and 2, check to see if anyone has found a method that uses fewer moves.

You might then let students exchange and work on the sheep-and-goats problems they invented in Question 3.

Year 1 Blackline Masters

• •

This page in the Year 1 student book, copyright 2004, introduces students to the additional Problems of the Week.

More Problems of the Week

This appendix to the Year 1 textbook provides a set of Problems of the Week that supplement those earlier in the book. Here are comments on a few examples:

- *Magic Squares* and *Magic Triangles* both involve filling in grids with numbers to make certain sums all come out the same. Although you may have seen similar problems before, these will challenge your imagination and insight.

- *Tic-Tac-Toe and Friends* asks you to explore a familiar game from the perspective of strategy, then to take your analysis deeper by looking at more complex versions of this game.

- *Crossing Old Rivers* presents several problems that were written more than 1000 years ago but still have the capacity to intrigue problem solvers.

- *A Camel Messenger* is a variation on *POW 13: Corey Camel.* Corey's friend Dory has a somewhat different mission, and your task is to help her accomplish it as efficiently as possible.

POW A

Polyominoes

You may have played a game called *dominoes*. A domino is shaped like a 2-by-1 rectangle, with a certain number of dots on each half of the piece. The figure at the right shows a "5, 6 domino."

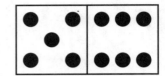

The domino shape is an example of a *polyomino,* which is a figure formed by putting identical squares together in a manner similar to dominoes.

For instance, this figure is a polyomino using six squares.

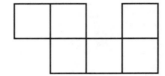

Polyominoes must follow these two rules.

- Rule 1: Each square must share a complete side with at least one other square.

- Rule 2: If two squares share part of a side, they must share the entire side.

The next figures are not considered polyominoes. The first figure violates Rule 1 because the first square does not have a side in common with either of the other two. The second figure violates Rule 2. Although each square has a complete side in common with another square, the upper squares share only *partial* sides with the lower squares.

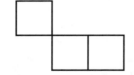

This figure violates Rule 1
(but fits Rule 2).

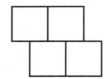

This figure violates Rule 2
(but fits Rule 1).

Continued on next page

Polyominoes are classified by how many squares they contain, using names based on common numerical prefixes.

- A domino contains 2 squares.
- A triomino contains 3 squares.
- A tetromino contains 4 squares.
- A pentomino contains 5 squares.
- A hexomino contains 6 squares.

And so on.

When Are They the Same?

Two polyominoes are considered to be the same if you can slide, rotate, and/or flip one of them so that it exactly coincides with the other. For example, these two tetrominoes are considered the same. You can't get them to line up just by rotating them, but if you flip one over, you can rotate it to match the other.

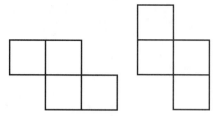

From the perspective of shape, dominoes are not very interesting; they are all the same. But triominoes come in two different shapes. Every triomino is the same shape as one of these.

The straight triomino   The corner triomino

Your Tasks

Here are several challenges related to polyominoes.

1. Find all the different tetrominoes.

2. Find all the different pentominoes.

Continued on next page

3. In "checkerboard polyominoes," each square is either black or white, with adjacent squares of opposite colors, as if the polyomino had been cut out of a checkerboard. Two checkerboard polyominoes are considered the same only if they are the same shape *and* their color patterns match.

These two figures are the same shape, but they have different color patterns. As checkerboard triominoes, they are different.

a. How many different checkerboard triominoes are there altogether (including the two shown)?

b. How many different checkerboard tetrominoes are there?

c. How many different checkerboard pentominoes are there?

4. *Extra Challenge:* Find all the different hexominoes, and then find all the different checkerboard hexominoes.

Write-up

1. *Problem Statement:* Include an explanation, in your own words, of what a polyomino is and what it means for two polyominoes to be the same.

2. *Process:* Describe any system you used or developed for finding *all* the polyominoes of a given size and explain how you made sure not to include any duplicates.

3. *Solution:* Show the sets of polyominoes you found. You may want to use grid paper to make your diagrams.

4. *Extensions:* Are there other special kinds of polyominoes (similar to checkerboard polyominoes) that you might investigate?

5. *Evaluation*

● ●

POW B   *Magic Squares*

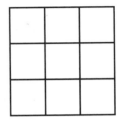

For centuries, people throughout the world have played with the challenge of finding magic squares. The simplest example involves a 3-by-3 grid. The task is to place the numbers 1 through 9 in the grid, one number per box (using each number exactly once), so that the sum of three-in-a-row in any direction—vertical, horizontal, or diagonal—is the same.

1. a. Find a solution to this magic square problem.

   b. Describe the insights you found in searching for your solution.

2. Find *all* the solutions to this magic square problem.

3. Prove that the solutions you found in Question 2 are the only ones possible. (*Suggestion:* Begin by proving what the middle number must be.)

4. Why is the 3-by-3 grid considered the simplest magic square to study? Why not a 2-by-2 grid (using the numbers 1 through 4)?

5. The next case involves the 4-by-4 grid at the right. A magic square for this grid involves ten sums: four vertical sums, four horizontal sums, and two diagonal sums.

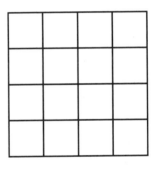

   a. Suppose you were to place the numbers 1 through 16 in this grid, one number per box, so that the ten four-in-a-row sums are all the same. What would those sums be? Explain how you can be sure.

   b. Make a "partly magic" square by placing the numbers 1 through 16 in the grid so the row sums are all the same.

   c. (Hard!) Construct a "mostly magic" square—one with sums of rows and columns all equal—or, even better, construct a "completely magic" square, in which all ten sums are the same. (In either case, use each of the numbers 1 through 16 exactly once.)

6. Suppose you have a "completely magic" square for the 4-by-4 grid. How can you use it to create more such squares?

Continued on next page

Write-up

1. *Problem Statement*

2. *Process*

3. *Solution:* Where possible, give all the solutions to a given magic square problem.

4. *Extensions:* Pose your own extension questions. You don't necessarily have to solve the extensions you suggest, so you can pose questions that are as challenging as you like!

5. *Evaluation*

• •

POW C   *Crossing the Bridge*

Four people want to cross a bridge. They are all at the same end of the bridge. But it's dark and they have only one flashlight, and at most, two people at a time can use the flashlight.

So they have to go across one or two at a time. Until everyone is across, someone must bring the flashlight back to the others. (The flashlight must be walked back and forth; it cannot be thrown or transported in any other way.)

To make things more complicated, the four people walk at different speeds.

- Ally needs only 1 minute to cross the bridge.
- Brian needs 2 minutes to cross the bridge.
- Carlos needs 5 minutes to cross the bridge.
- Doretha needs 10 minutes to cross the bridge.

If two people are crossing together, they go at the speed of the slower person.

The Challenge

How should the four people cross so that they all end up on the other side in the shortest possible amount of time? What are all the options for achieving this minimum time?

Write-up

1. *Process:* Keep track of what you do as you work on this problem. Indicate any places you got stuck or thought you had the "minimum time" when it turned out there was a better solution.

2. *Solution:* Give as many options for achieving the minimum as you can find, and explain why you think you have them all.

3. *Evaluation*

POW D

Magic Triangles

You may be familiar with magic squares, which involve placing numbers in a square array so that certain sums are all equal. These problems involve a similar idea with triangles.

1. This triangle has nine empty circles. Your task is to place the numbers 1 through 9 in these nine circles (using each number exactly once) so that the sum for each side of the triangle is the same.

   How many solutions can you find? What are they?

   Warning: There is more than one possible solution, and different solutions can involve different sums!

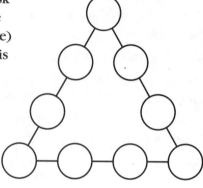

2. The double triangle here is composed of two triangles, with one turned upside-down and placed on top of the other. Because there are 12 circles, you will use the numbers 1 through 12, again using each exactly once.

   In this problem, not only must the sum be the same for each four-in-a-row, but also the vertices of the triangles (the six outermost circles) must combine to give that same sum.

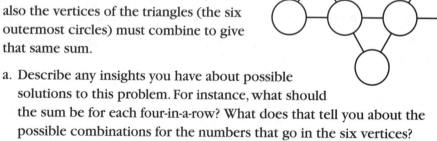

   a. Describe any insights you have about possible solutions to this problem. For instance, what should the sum be for each four-in-a-row? What does that tell you about the possible combinations for the numbers that go in the six vertices?

   b. Find a solution to this double-triangle problem.

   c. Find *all* the solutions to this problem. (Two solutions should be considered the same if you can get one from the other by rotating and/or flipping.)

Continued on next page

Write-up

1. *Process:* Describe any systems you used or developed to help you find the solutions.

2. *Solution:* Be sure to indicate whether you think you have all the solutions, and why you think so.

3. *Extensions:* Make up a magic-shape problem of your own. State the problem clearly, give all the solutions you find, and explain why you think you have all the solutions.

4. *Evaluation*

From *The Penguin Book of Curious and Interesting Puzzles,* by David Wells (London, England: Penguin, 1992). Copyright © 1992 by Penguin Books Ltd. Adapted with permission.

POW E   *Tic-Tac-Toe and Friends*

In the game of tic-tac-toe, players take turns making marks on a 3-by-3 board. Each mark goes in one of the nine squares. One person is **X** and the other is **O**, and the goal is to get three of your mark in a row, in any direction.

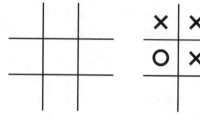

A blank tic-tac-toe board

O can block X in only one direction, so X will win.

In the second diagram, a game is under way, and it is **O**'s turn. But **X** can win in the next round by marking either of two squares. Because **O** can't mark both of them, **X** will be able to win whatever choice **O** makes.

1. Analyze the game tic-tac-toe. Suppose **X** makes the first mark. Is there a way that **X** can be sure to win? Is there a way that **O** can prevent **X** from winning? Which square should **X** mark to make things as difficult as possible for **O**?

2. Suppose the board is extended to four by four.

   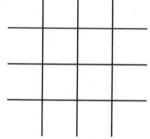

   a. If a player still needs to get only three marks in a row, what happens? Can one player guarantee a win? If so, how should that player proceed? If not, how can each player prevent the other from winning?

   b. What if a player needs four marks in a row on this board? Is it possible for one player to guarantee a win? If so, how should that player proceed? If not, how can each player prevent the other from winning? (*Hint:* There are really only three opening moves that you need to consider. Why?)

3. What if the board is unlimited? Here are some questions to explore for this situation.

   a. Show that on an unlimited board, the first player can get three marks in a row within just three moves no matter what the second player does.

   b. Can the first player get four marks in a row no matter what the second player does? If so, how should the first player proceed? How should the first player respond to different moves by the second player?

Continued on next page

Write-up

1. *Problem Statement:* You do not need to explain how the games are played. Instead, put into words what your goal is in working on this problem.

2. *Process:* You may want to attach some of your scratchwork from your efforts on this problem to illustrate how you went about working on it.

3. *Solution:* Your solution will be an analysis of what happens in each game.

4. *Evaluation*

POW F   *Crossing Old Rivers*

"How do you get them across the river?" That is the question in many old puzzles.

These problems are taken from a work called *Propositiones ad acuendos juvenes,* which means "Propositions to sharpen the young." This is the earliest known European collection of mathematical puzzles. It was written in a monastery in Augsberg (in what is now Germany) about the year 1000 CE. It is thought to be the work of Alcuin (ca. 732–804), an English scholar who spent much of his life at the court of Emperor Charlemagne.

In each of these problems, look for a solution that involves the smallest possible number of steps.

1. Three men, each with a sister, need to cross a river. At the river, they find only a small boat, in which only two of them can cross at a time. How can all six get across?

    The challenge is that the men are very jealous and protective. Each insists that his sister cannot be left with any man present, even for a moment, unless he, the brother, is there.

Continued on next page

2. A man and a woman, each the weight of a loaded cart, with two children who, combined, weigh as much as a loaded cart, have to cross a river. The boat can only carry a weight equal to one loaded cart. How should they get across? Assume that a child is able to row.

3. A man wants to take a wolf, a goat, and a cabbage across the river. The only boat he can find will carry only two of them (the man and one other) at a time. How can he get them all across safely?

The challenge is that if the wolf and the goat are together without the man, the wolf will eat the goat, and if the goat and the cabbage are together without the man, the goat will eat the cabbage. The wolf doesn't eat cabbage.

Write-up

1. *Process:* Describe the attempts you made on each problem. Include comments on how your work on any one of these problems was helpful on others.

2. *Solution:* State each solution clearly and in detail. Also indicate if you think there are other solutions and what they are. If possible, demonstrate that you have solved each problem using the fewest possible steps.

3. *Evaluation*

From *The Penguin Book of Curious and Interesting Puzzles,* by David Wells (London, England: Penguin, 1992). Copyright © 1992 by Penguin Books Ltd. Adapted with permission.

● ●

POW G   *Exposed*

Imagine that each layer of this step pyramid is made
from identical, cube-shaped blocks of stone. The
bottom layer has seven rows of stones with
seven stones in each row. The next layer
has five rows of stones with five stones
in each row. The third layer has three rows
of stones with three stones in each row.
And the top layer is a single stone.

1. Some of the stones are completely hidden in this arrangement, so they are
   not exposed to rain, wind, and the other elements.

   a. How many stones are exposed?

   b. How can you explain your result without counting the stones layer by
      layer?

2. Each stone is shaped like a cube, so each has six faces, although not all the
   faces of each stone are exposed. If there were a big rainstorm and all the
   exposed faces got wet, how many stones would have one wet face? Two wet
   faces? Three wet faces? Four wet faces? Five wet faces? Six wet faces?

3. Now imagine a larger version of this structure, in which the bottom layer has
   25 rows of stones with 25 stones in each row. The next layer, centered on the
   first, has 23 rows of stones with 23 stones in each row. The next layer has
   21 rows of stones with 21 stones in each row, and so on.

   a. How many layers does this structure have?

   b. How many exposed stones does this structure have?

   c. How many stones in this structure have one exposed face? Two exposed
      faces? Three exposed faces? Four exposed faces? Five exposed faces? Six
      exposed faces?

4. How can you generalize your results from Questions 1 through 3?

Continued on next page

© 2004 Interactive Mathematics Program®

Super Challenge

Questions 1 through 4 involve only the *exposed* stones. How many stones are there altogether, both exposed and hidden? Look for a formula or pattern based on the number of layers in the pile.

Write-up

1. *Problem Statement:* Express in your own words the questions that you are trying to answer in this problem. You do not need to describe the structures themselves.

2. *Process:* What counting techniques did you use? How did you work on developing generalizations? What other specific examples did you examine?

3. *Solution:* Give numerical values for the specific examples, show how you got them, and give any general formulas you developed.

4. *Extensions:* What other questions might you ask about such structures?

5. *Evaluation*

● ●

POW H

Egyptian Fractions

Mathematicians in ancient Egypt knew about fractions, but they had a peculiar limitation. They worked only with *unit fractions* (fractions with a numerator of 1), such as $\frac{1}{3}$ or $\frac{1}{12}$.

The easy way to get other fractions from unit fractions is by repeated addition. For example, you could also write $\frac{3}{5}$ as $\frac{1}{5} + \frac{1}{5} + \frac{1}{5}$. But the Egyptians made things more complicated (from our perspective) because they preferred not to repeat the same fraction. If they wanted to talk about what we would write as $\frac{3}{5}$, they might express it as $\frac{1}{2} + \frac{1}{10}$, using two distinct unit fractions.

Fractions Rewritten

Work with *proper fractions* (fractions less than 1) that have denominators up to 10 and numerators greater than 1. Consider only fractions that have been simplified, so that the numerator and denominator have no common factor other than 1.

1. Write every such fraction as a sum of distinct unit fractions. (In some cases, you may need to use more than two terms to get the desired sum.)

No More Than the Numerator

As noted earlier, if you are allowed to use the same unit fraction more than once, you can write $\frac{3}{5}$ as $\frac{1}{5} + \frac{1}{5} + \frac{1}{5}$. There are three terms, because the numerator of is 3. Similarly, you can write $\frac{7}{11}$ as a sum of seven terms, each equal to $\frac{1}{11}$, or write $\frac{13}{46}$ as a sum of 13 terms, each equal to $\frac{1}{46}$, and so on. You never need more terms in the sum than the numerator of the fraction you are rewriting.

Continued on next page

But under the ancient Egyptian rules, you are prohibited from using the same fraction more than once.

2. Show that any proper fraction with a numerator of 2 and an odd denominator can be written as the sum of two distinct unit fractions. (*Suggestion:* Do some examples first and look for patterns.)

3. (Harder!) Show that any proper fraction with a numerator of 3 can be written as the sum of at most three distinct unit fractions.

It turns out that you can write *any* proper fraction as a sum of distinct unit fractions so that the number of terms is no more than the numerator and is possibly fewer. Questions 2 and 3 are specific cases of this.

4. What insights do you have about why this general statement is true?

Write-up

1. *Problem Statement*

2. *Process:* For example, describe how you went about finding the expressions called for in this activity. Was it simply random trial and error, or did you find some techniques to make your work easier?

3. *Solution*

   a. On Question 1, give the specific expressions, and give more than one if you found more than one.

   b. On Questions 2 and 3, give any examples you used to get ideas, but also try to provide a general procedure and justify your procedure.

   c. On Question 4, describe any insights you had, but also describe what issues you were unable to resolve or what you think would be needed to be able to completely justify the general statement.

4. *Evaluation*

From *The Penguin Book of Curious and Interesting Puzzles,* by David Wells (London, England: Penguin, 1992). Copyright © 1992 by Penguin Books Ltd. Adapted with permission.

● ●

POW 1

Pieces at Peace

The chess piece called a *queen* can move in any one direction on the board—vertically, horizontally, or along a diagonal.

If there are no other pieces in the way, the queen can move as far as it likes in any one direction. For example, a queen located at the **Q** in the diagram can move to any square marked with an **X**.

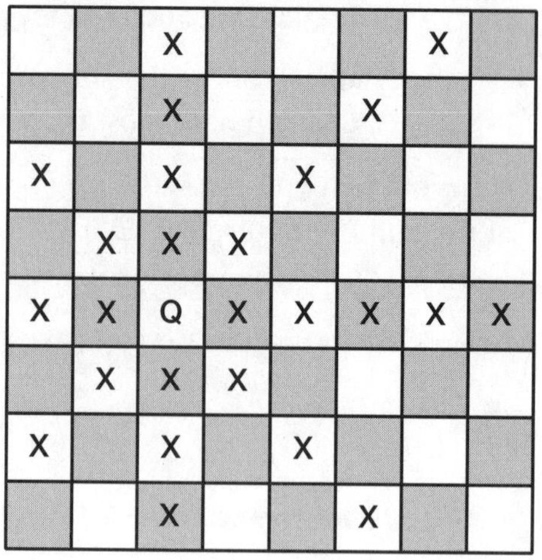

But if there is another piece in one of those squares, the queen can attack and remove the piece.

The question is

How many queens can be "at peace" on a checkerboard?

In other words, starting from an empty board, how many queens can you place so that no queen can attack any other queen? The game of chess uses a standard 8-by-8 checkerboard, but this question can be posed for boards of other sizes. As you might guess, the number of queens that can be at peace depends on the size of the board.

1. Explain why the number of queens that can be placed on a board and still be at peace cannot be more than the number of rows.

2. For a 2-by-2 checkerboard, explain why only one queen can be at peace.

3. Can you place three queens on a 3-by-3 checkerboard and have them be at peace? Explain why or why not.

4. Can you place four queens on a 4-by-4 checkerboard and have them be at peace? How many queens can be at peace on a 5-by-5 checkerboard? Justify your answers.

5. On a standard 8-by-8 checkerboard, can you place eight queens and have them be at peace? Explain why or why not.

Continued on next page

6. Answer similar questions for these other pieces in the game of chess.

   • The bishop, which moves only on diagonals

   • The rook, which moves only vertically or horizontally

   • The knight, which moves in an **L** shape: either two squares horizontally and one vertically or two squares vertically and one horizontally

The **X**'s in this diagram indicate the eight places to which a knight located at the **K** might move. (The knight can move to its destination whether or not squares along the way are occupied.)

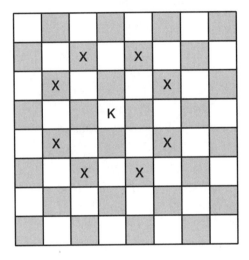

Write-up

1. *Problem Statement*

2. *Process:* Describe any materials you used or techniques you tried to help you find solutions.

3. *Solution:* Provide diagrams to show specific solutions you found.

4. *Extensions:* Include here any work you did on Question 6 as well as any other questions you think are worth examining.

5. *Evaluation*

From *The Penguin Book of Curious and Interesting Puzzles,* by David Wells (London, England: Penguin, 1992). Copyright © 1992 by Penguin Books Ltd. Adapted with permission.

POW J   *A Camel Messenger*

Dory is a fictitious camel who lives on bananas. She eats one banana during each and every mile she walks. She can carry at most 1000 bananas at a time.

Dory is being sent to deliver a message. The trip will take her to a place that is 1000 miles across the desert. She needs to get there, deliver her message, and then return home. She knows there are no bananas to be found along the route in either direction, but she also knows that she can leave bananas safely at any place along her route.

What is the minimum number of bananas that Dory needs to have at the start of her journey to reach her destination and return using only those bananas?

Write-up

1. *Problem Statement*

2. *Process*

3. *Solution:* Include here any explanation you can provide for why you think you have found the absolute minimum number of bananas that Dory needs.

4. *Evaluation*

This problem was suggested by Professor Terence Gaffney of Northeastern University, Boston, Massachusetts. He created the problem while teaching IMP to college students.

• •

Year 2 Blackline Masters

This page in the Year 2 student book, copyright 2004, introduces students to the additional Problems of the Week.

More POWs

More Problems of the Week

This appendix to the Year 2 textbook provides a set of Problems of the Week that supplement those earlier in the book. Here are comments on a few examples:

- *Last Loses and Other Nim Variations* picks up where Year 1's *POW 6: Linear Nim* left off. The focus in this problem is on finding the best strategy.

- *Old Number Puzzles* contains three problems that are nearly 2000 years old. And the fourth problem asks the life span of the creator of the first three!

- *Triangle Variety, Geoboard Squares,* and *Geoboard Triangle Areas* all involve polygons on a geoboard. Get out your rubber bands!

POW A
Last Loses and Other Nim Variations

In the game of Linear Nim, two players take turns crossing out marks on a page according to specific rules. The person who crosses out the last mark is the winner. Here's how a particular form of Linear Nim works.

Play begins with ten marks on a piece of paper, as shown here.

Each player, in turn, crosses off one, two, or three marks. (It doesn't matter which marks are crossed off.)

Play continues until the players have crossed out all the marks. The player who crosses off the last mark is the winner.

Last Loses

1. Suppose you change the rules of the game so that the player who crosses off the last mark is the loser.

   a. Using the ten-mark starting situation, which player can guarantee a win (the first player or the second)? What strategy should that player use?

   b. Suppose you change the number of marks at the start of the game. Now who should win? How does the number of marks at the start of the game influence which player wins?

At Least Two

2. Suppose you use the original rule that the player who crosses off the last mark wins, but you require that each player cross off at least two marks at every turn (but still no more than three). If there is one mark left, then the next player cannot move, and the game is considered a tie.

Continued on next page

a. If the game starts with ten marks, what is likely to happen if the players are good at the game?

b. Suppose you change the number of marks at the start of the game. How does the outcome depend on the number of marks you start with?

More Variations

3. Explore other variations of this game. For example,

- Combine the changes described so that the player who takes the last mark loses and each player must take at least two marks at every turn.

- Change the maximum number of marks allowed per turn.

- Use a minimum number of marks per turn greater than two.

In each of your variations, examine how the outcome depends on the number of marks at the start of the game.

Write-up

1. *Problem Statement:* Put into words what your goal is in working on this problem. You do not need to explain how the games are played.

2. *Process:* Describe how you analyzed the different variations.

3. *Solution:* Describe specific cases and any generalizations you developed.

4. *Extensions:* Include your work from "More Variations" here.

5. *Evaluation*

• •

POW B   *Old Number Puzzles*

Diophantos was a Greek mathematician who lived at about 250 CE. He was especially interested in integer solutions to special kinds of equations, and such problems are sometimes called *Diophantine equations*.

Here are three examples from Book I of his work, which was called *Arithmetica*.

1. What number must be added to 100 and to 20 (the same number to each) so that the sums are in the ratio 3:1?

2. Two numbers are such that if the first receives 30 from the second, their ratio is 2:1. But if the second receives 50 from the first, their ratio is 1:3. What are the numbers?

3. The sums of four numbers, omitting each number in turn, are 22, 24, 27, and 20. What are the numbers?

Continued on next page

And speaking of Diophantos, here's a problem *about* him, credited to Metrodorus from about 500 CE:

4. This tomb contains Diophantos. Ah, how great a marvel! The tomb tells scientifically the measure of his life. He was a boy for the sixth part of his life, and adding a twelfth part to this, his beard began to grow. He was married after a seventh part, and five years after his marriage, his son was born. But the child, after attaining the measure of half his father's life, died. After consoling his grief with this science of numbers for four years, Diophantos's life ended.

How long did Diophantos live?

Note: When the problem says that the child attained "the measure of half his father's life," it means half of the father's total life, not just half the father's age at the time the child died.

Beyond the Originals

The problems above are stated using specific numbers. For instance, Question 1 uses the numbers 100 and 20 and the ratio 3:1. Explore how these problems might be different if you changed these numbers. Would they still have solutions? Would they have more than one solution? How would the answers to the two questions just stated depend on the specific numbers you used?

Write-up

1. *Process:* Describe any equations or organized systems you used for finding your solutions.

2. *Solutions:* Show why your solutions fit the problems.

3. *Extensions:* Include your work from "Beyond the Originals."

4. *Evaluation*

POW C   *A Square in a Square*

You may recall Leslie from the "border problems" in Year 1. She was interested in square gardens.

Now Leslie's younger sister Elissa wants to use part of Leslie's garden. In fact, Elissa wants a square section in the corner of Leslie's garden. So the two of them sit down with pencil and paper to sketch out some possibilities and to see how much area Leslie would have left if she gave part of the space to Elissa.

For example, in this sketch, Leslie's square garden is 4 feet on each side and Elissa gets the shaded square, which is 2 feet on each side.

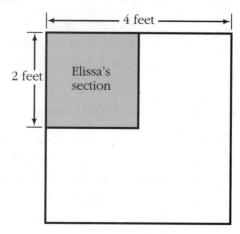

In this case, the original garden has an area of 16 square feet ($4^2 = 16$), and Elissa's section has an area of 4 square feet ($2^2 = 4$), so Leslie is left with an area of 12 square feet.

They begin to wonder what other possible areas Leslie could end up with. Can you help? Assume that they use only whole numbers for the lengths of the sides.

1. Begin by examining the numbers 1 through 20. For each number, try to find sizes for the two squares so that Leslie ends up with that many square feet of area. (For instance, the example above shows that Leslie can have 12 square feet by starting with a 4-by-4 square and giving Elissa a 2-by-2 square.)

   Keep track of all the possibilities you find in each case.

2. Look for patterns and generalize. Determine which whole numbers (not just those from 1 to 20) represent areas that Leslie can end up with and which do not. Justify your conclusions.

Continued on next page

Write-up

1. *Problem Statement:* State the problem in a pure "mathematical" form without reference to gardens or individuals.

2. *Process:* Include how you gathered and organized information to help you solve the problem.

3. *Solution:* Give the specific results you found for Question 1 and any general principles or patterns you saw. If you can, explain your patterns.

4. *Extensions*

5. *Evaluation*

● ●

POW D   *Triangle Variety*

In other activities, you looked for geoboard triangles with an area of exactly 2 units or fitting other conditions. In this activity, your exploration is more open-ended. You will examine geoboards of different sizes. As usual, a "geoboard triangle" must have its vertices at geoboard pegs.

The case of a 2-peg-by-2-peg geoboard is simple; all the triangles you can make are congruent. There are four possible triangles, shown here, but they are all congruent to one another.

So you need only one of them for a "complete set of noncongruent triangles" for a geoboard of this size.

Three-by-Three

The case of a 3-peg-by-3-peg geoboard is more complex. There are many triangles that can be made on such a geoboard. Some are congruent to each other, so they don't count as different. For instance, in these triangles, A and B are congruent to each other. But triangles C and D are different from A and B and different from each other, so the examples here represent three different triangles.

A   B   C   D

There are other triangles possible on this geoboard that are not congruent to any of the ones above, so here is your first challenge.

1. Find a complete set of noncongruent triangles on a 3-peg-by-3-peg geoboard, and show that your set is complete.

Continued on next page

Here is another challenge.

2. Determine the total number of triangles on this geoboard, counting each one separately, even if it is congruent to others. (*Hint:* A triangle has three vertices. There are nine pegs on the board. What are the possibilities?)

Four-by-Four

Here are your final challenges for this activity.

3. Find a complete set of noncongruent triangles on a 4-peg-by-4-peg geoboard, and show that your set is complete.

4. Determine the total number of possible triangles on a 4-peg-by-4-peg geoboard.

Write-up

1. *Problem Statement:* Include an explanation of what "a complete set of noncongruent triangles" means.

2. *Process*

3. *Solution:* You will probably want to use grid paper to display the geoboard triangles. Indicate why you think you have all the distinct triangles on a given geoboard.

4. *Extensions*

5. *Evaluation*

POW E   *Geoboard Squares*

On a 2-peg–by–2-peg geoboard, there is only one way to make a square, as shown here.

But for larger geoboards, there is more variety.

For example, on a 3-peg–by–3-peg geoboard, there are three different sizes for squares, as illustrated here. (As usual, the vertices must be at geoboard pegs.)

The first case is not that interesting because it can be made on a smaller geoboard. So your focus in this problem will be on the number of *new* squares that can be formed at each stage as the geoboard is enlarged. For instance, you have just seen that for a 3-peg–by–3-peg geoboard, there are two new squares.

You should consider squares to be different only if they are different sizes. For instance, these two squares should be considered the same.

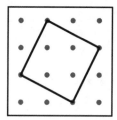 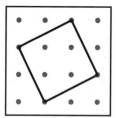

The Challenges

1. Consider geoboards of the next several sizes, at least through a 7-peg–by–7-peg geoboard, and determine the number of new, distinct squares that can be created at each stage.

Continued on next page

---

2. Develop a generalization for how many new squares can be formed on an N-peg-by-N-peg geoboard. For example, use your work in Question 1 to help you predict how many different squares can be formed on a 100-peg-by-100-peg geoboard that cannot be formed on a smaller geoboard. Explain why your generalization is correct.

3. (Harder!) Use your work from Question 2 to develop a formula or rule for the *total* number of squares that can be formed on an N-peg-by-N-peg geoboard, including those that can be formed on smaller geoboards.

Write-up

1. *Problem Statement*

2. *Process:* Describe how your work on Question 1 helped you develop ideas for Question 2.

3. *Solution:* Give the specific squares you found for the individual geoboards in Question 1, and then describe any observations or generalizations you were able to make based on those results.

4. *Extensions*

5. *Evaluation*

• •

POW F *Geoboard Triangle Areas*

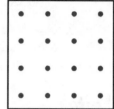

Think about the different triangles that can be formed with vertices at pegs on this 4-peg-by-4-peg geoboard.

If one side of a triangle is horizontal, then you can use that side as the base, and both the base and the height will be whole numbers. In that case, you can find the area fairly easily.

1. Find the possible areas for triangles that have a horizontal side and whose vertices are at pegs of this geoboard. Give at least one example for each possible area, and show that your list of possible areas is complete.

But if you don't insist on having a horizontal side, then there are other possible areas.

2. Find *all* the possible areas for triangles whose vertices are at pegs of a 4-peg-by-4-peg geoboard. Again, give at least one example for each possible area, and show that your list of possible areas is complete. (You need to give only areas that were not already included in your answer to Question 1.)

3. Answer Question 1 for this 5-peg-by-5-peg geoboard.

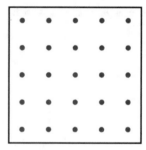

4. Answer Question 2 for this 5-peg-by-5-peg geoboard.

5. What do you predict would be the possible areas for triangles on a 6-peg-by-6-peg geoboard? What about larger geoboards? Explain your answers.

Write-up

1. *Problem Statement*

2. *Process*

3. *Solution:* Include diagrams for each area that you think is possible, and explain why you think no other areas are possible.

4. *Extensions*

5. *Evaluation*

POW G   *What's That Hat?*

In the saga of the great detective Sherlock Holmes, the Baker Street Irregulars were a group of young people who often acted as the eyes and ears for Holmes. Here's a test they once gave to candidates for the group.

Three candidates were told that they would be blindfolded and that a hat would be placed on the head of each one. Each hat could be either black or white.

At a signal, the blindfolds would be removed, and each candidate could see the hats of the other two. Anyone who saw a black hat was to raise his or her hand. The first to correctly deduce the color of his or her own hat and perfectly explain the deduction would be admitted.

Once the blindfolds had been put on, all three were given black hats. When the blindfolds were removed, all three raised their hands.

If you were one of the three candidates, would you be able to determine what color your hat was? How would you know? You may assume that the other two candidates are reasonably bright people.

Write-up

1. *Problem Statement*

2. *Process*

3. *Solution:* You need to explain how you could be *absolutely certain* of the color of your hat. Indicate why you need to use the assumption that "the other two candidates are reasonably bright people."

4. *Extensions:* How might you vary this problem? Would the variations you create have solutions?

5. *Evaluation*

Adapted from *Mathematical Puzzles,* by Geoffrey Mott-Smith (New York: Dover, 1954).

POW H   *Sheep and Goats*

Each square in the diagram represents a pen for an animal. Right now, six animals alternate—sheep, goat, sheep, goat, sheep, goat—in the first six pens, and pens 7 and 8 are empty.

The farmer wants to rearrange the animals so the sheep are all together and the goats are all together. But the animals don't like to be moved one at a time. The only way the farmer can get them to cooperate in going to new pens is to take two animals in adjacent pens (such as the sheep in pen 3 and the goat in pen 4) and move them together to the two empty pens. And the two animals being moved must stay in the same order they are in at the start.

For example, these diagrams show what happens if the farmer starts from the arrangement above and moves the animals in pens 3 and 4 to the two empty pens.

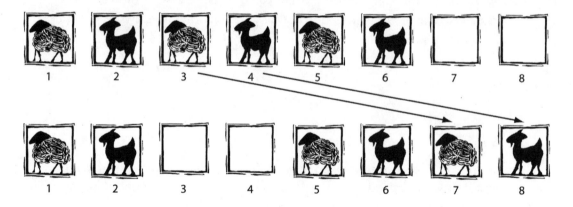

Continued on next page

1. Start from the original setup, and rearrange the animals so that the sheep end up in pens 1, 2, and 3 and the goats end up in pens 6, 7, and 8. Do this in as few moves as possible.

2. Start from the original setup, and rearrange the animals so that the goats end up in pens 1, 2, and 3 and the sheep end up in pens 6, 7, and 8. Again, do this in as few moves as possible.

3. Make up your own sheep-and-goats problems and solve them. You might consider more pens, more animals, and so on.

Write-up

1. *Problem Statement*

2. *Process:* Describe any materials you used to help you find your solutions.

3. *Solution:* Give your step-by-step process for each of Questions 1 and 2, and indicate what makes you think you have done the rearrangements in as few moves as possible.

4. *Extensions:* Include your work from Question 3.

5. *Evaluation*

• •

Notes

Notes

Notes

Key Curriculum Press
Innovators in Mathematics Education

Comment Form

Please take a moment to provide us with feedback about this book. We are eager to read any comments or suggestions you may have. Once you've filled out this form, simply fold it along the dotted lines and drop it in the mail. We'll pay the postage. Thank you!

Your Name _____

School _____

School Address _____

City/State/Zip _____

Phone _____

Book Title _____

Please list any comments you have about this book.

_____

_____

_____

_____

_____

_____

_____

_____

_____

_____

_____

Do you have any suggestions for improving the student or teacher material?

_____

_____

_____

_____

_____

_____

To request a catalog, or place an order, call us toll free at 800-995-MATH, or send a fax to 800-541-2242.
For more information, visit Key's website at www.keypress.com.

Please detach page, fold on lines and tape edge.

NO POSTAGE
NECESSARY
IF MAILED
IN THE
UNITED STATES

BUSINESS REPLY MAIL
FIRST CLASS   PERMIT NO. 338   OAKLAND, CA

POSTAGE WILL BE PAID BY ADDRESSEE

KEY CURRICULUM PRESS
1150 65TH STREET
EMERYVILLE CA 94608-9740